COUNTRY 🌐 PROFILES

THE
PHILIPPINES

BY ALICIA Z. KLEPEIS

BELLWETHER MEDIA • MINNEAPOLIS, MN

Blastoff! Discovery launches a new mission: reading to learn. Filled with facts and features, each book offers you an exciting new world to explore!

BLASTOFF! UNIVERSE

BLASTOFF! Beginners — GRADE K

BLASTOFF! READERS — GRADES 1-3

BLASTOFF! DISCOVERY — GRADE 4

This edition first published in 2021 by Bellwether Media, Inc.

No part of this publication may be reproduced in whole or in part without written permission of the publisher.
For information regarding permission, write to Bellwether Media, Inc., Attention: Permissions Department,
6012 Blue Circle Drive, Minnetonka, MN 55343.

Library of Congress Cataloging-in-Publication Data

Names: Klepeis, Alicia, 1971- author.
Title: The Philippines / by Alicia Z. Klepeis.
Description: Minneapolis, MN : Bellwether Media, Inc., 2021. |
    Series: Blastoff! Discovery : country profiles | Includes
    bibliographical references and index. | Audience: Ages 7-13 |
    Audience: Grades 4-6 | Summary: "Engaging images accompany
    information about the Philippines. The combination of high-interest
    subject matter and narrative text is intended for students in grades
    3 through 8"– Provided by publisher.
Identifiers: LCCN 2020001632 (print) | LCCN 2020001633
    (ebook) | ISBN 9781644872550 (library binding) | ISBN
    9781681037189 (ebook)
Subjects: LCSH: Philippines–Juvenile literature.
Classification: LCC DS655 .K54 2021 (print) | LCC DS655 (ebook)
    | DDC 959.9–dc23
LC record available at https://lccn.loc.gov/2020001632
LC ebook record available at https://lccn.loc.gov/2020001633

Editor: Kieran Downs   Designer: Brittany McIntosh

Printed in the United States of America, North Mankato, MN.

TABLE OF CONTENTS

BEAUTIFUL BOHOL

CHOCOLATE HILLS

It is a hot morning on the island of Bohol. A group of **tourists** arrives at the Chocolate Hills. These grassy hills turn brown during the dry months. They look like chocolate drops! After exploring for a bit, the group takes a boat tour down the Loboc River. Colorful sunbirds flit about as the tourists cruise past palm trees.

4

OTHER TOP SITES

BANAUE RICE TERRACES

HUNDRED ISLANDS NATIONAL PARK

PUERTO-PRINCESA SUBTERRANEAN RIVER NATIONAL PARK

SAN AGUSTIN CHURCH

Next, the visitors drive to the Philippine Tarsier **Sanctuary**. They spot the tiny, bug-eyed **primates** eating insects while moving about in their tree homes. The group ends their day watching the sunset on a nearby beach. Welcome to the Philippines!

The Philippines is located in southeast Asia. The country covers 115,831 square miles (300,000 square kilometers). This **archipelago** in the Pacific Ocean has over 7,000 islands. Mindanao and Luzon are the biggest of the country's 11 main islands. Manila, the capital, is on Luzon.

No nations directly border the Philippines. The country is about 500 miles (805 kilometers) from the coast of **mainland** Asia. The South China Sea lies to the north and west. The Sulu Sea lies to the southwest. The waters of the Celebes Sea wash against the country's southern coast. Waves from the Philippine Sea hit the country's eastern shores.

SOUTH CHINA SEA

PHILIPPINE
SEA

LUZON

MANILA

THE
PHILIPPINES

CEBU CITY

SULU SEA

ZAMBOANGA

MINDANAO

DAVAO

MALAYSIA

CELEBES SEA

7

LANDSCAPE AND CLIMATE

The islands of the Philippines are mountainous. **Rain forests** cover many of the peaks. Some mountains are **volcanoes**, and over 20 are active. The Cordillera Central stands in northern Luzon. On Mindanao, the Diuata Mountains run along the eastern coast. The Cagayan and Agusan Rivers wind through valleys between ranges. Most islands feature low, coastal **plains** near the seas.

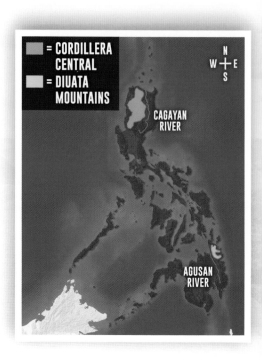

= CORDILLERA CENTRAL
= DIUATA MOUNTAINS

CAGAYAN RIVER

AGUSAN RIVER

A PINK BEACH

Great Santa Cruz Island has a beach with pink sand. Its color comes from the mixture of white sand and the crushed red coral that washes ashore.

CAMIGUIN ISLAND

MANILA

Average seasonal highs and lows

JANUARY
HIGH: 85 °F (29 °C)
LOW: 75 °F (24 °C)

APRIL
HIGH: 92 °F (33 °C)
LOW: 80 °F (27 °C)

JULY
HIGH: 88 °F (31 °C)
LOW: 78 °F (26 °C)

OCTOBER
HIGH: 88 °F (31 °C)
LOW: 78 °F (26 °C)

°F = degrees Fahrenheit
°C = degrees Celsius

The Philippines has a **tropical monsoonal** climate. Temperatures are warm all year long. Seasonal winds create a wet and dry season. The wet season brings heavy rains and **typhoons** from June to November. The dry season is from December to May.

The building of cities and farms has caused the rain forests of the Philippines to shrink. But the country is rich with wildlife. Catlike common palm civets feed on berries, insects, and rodents as parrots fly overhead. Wild pigs, deer, tarsiers, and bats are also found in Filipino forests. The Philippines is home to a huge variety of reptiles such as pythons and Philippine sailfin lizards.

Tiger sharks and green turtles swim among the country's **coral reefs**. Seabirds search for fish to eat. More than 2,000 species of fish make their homes in the Philippines' warm waters.

VISAYAN WARTY PIG

TIGER SHARK

PHILIPPINE TARSIER

FLYING FROGS

The harlequin flying frog is one of many types of flying frogs that live in the Philippines. Their webbed toes and fingers enable them to glide or leap from tree to tree.

COMMON
PALM CIVET

COMMON
PALM CIVET

Life Span: **up to 22 years**
Red List Status: **least concern**

common palm civet range = ■

LEAST CONCERN	NEAR THREATENED	VULNERABLE	ENDANGERED	CRITICALLY ENDANGERED	EXTINCT IN THE WILD	EXTINCT

More than 109 million people live in the Philippines.
Over seven out of ten Filipinos live on Luzon and Mindanao.
Filipinos come from many different **ethnic** groups. Around one
out of four belong to the Tagalog group. Filipinos may also
belong to the Bisaya, Cebuano, Ilocano, Bikol, or other groups.

The Philippines does not have an official religion. But most Filipinos are Roman Catholic Christians. Smaller groups of people practice other religions including Islam and Buddhism. The country's official languages are Filipino and English. However, people speak different **dialects** of Filipino such as Tagalog or Waray-Waray.

FAMOUS FACE

Name: Manny Pacquiao
Birthday: December 17, 1978
Hometown: Kibawe, Philippines
Famous for: Winner of major world boxing titles in a record eight different weight classes who also served in the Philippine House of Representatives and as a senator of the Philippines

SPEAK FILIPINO

ENGLISH	FILIPINO	HOW TO SAY IT
hello	kumusta	koo-moos-TAH
goodbye	paalam	pah-AH-lahm
please	paki	pah-KEE
thank you	salamat	sah-LAH-mat
yes	oo	OH-oh
no	hindi	heen-DEE

MANILA

Just under half of all Filipinos live in **urban** areas. Metro Manila is one of the country's largest urban areas. More than 13 million people live there. People in cities may live in apartments or single-family homes. Some also live in **shantytowns**. These crowded areas usually do not have plumbing or trash pickup. City travel is often by bus, taxi, or private car.

JAZZY JEEPNEYS

A common form of transportation in the Philippines is the jeepney. These minibuses are famous for their decorated paint jobs.

NIPA HUTS

A typical house in the countryside is a nipa hut. It is made of bamboo with a palm leaf roof. Animals, bicycles, and motorcycles are popular ways to get around in **rural** areas.

15

PAGMAMANO

From the earliest age, Filipinos are taught respect. One respectful **tradition** is called *pagmamano*. In this gesture, a younger person taps the back of an elder person's hand on their forehead. This tradition is common among rural Catholic Filipinos.

Western-style clothing is common in the Philippines. However, people in more remote areas sometimes wear traditional clothing. Muslim men and women on Mindanao may wear a garment called a *malong*. This brightly colored cloth tube can be worn many different ways.

MALONGS

Children in the Philippines begin school at age 5. Elementary education includes kindergarten through sixth grade. Junior high school consists of seventh through tenth grade. Students in senior high school can focus on academics, sports, arts and design, or **vocational** training. Those who complete secondary school may continue studying at colleges or universities.

Over half of all Filipinos have **service jobs**. Some work in national parks, hotels, or hospitals. About one out of ten people have jobs in tourism. Filipino workers **manufacture** products like communications equipment or clothing. Farmers grow rice, corn, and sugarcane. Many people also make a living by fishing.

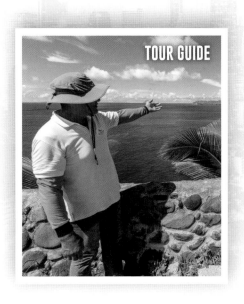

TOUR GUIDE

COCONUT CRAZE

Around the world, the sales of coconut products are growing fast. The Philippines is the world's second-largest producer of coconuts.

BASKETBALL

The most popular sport in the Philippines is basketball. It is common for cities to have their own courts. Filipinos also enjoy watching both local and professional basketball games. Boxing, badminton, and soccer are also well-liked sports.

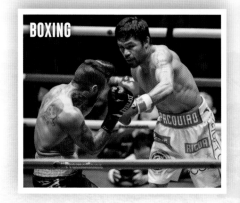

BOXING

In their free time, young Filipinos often play video games. Playing card games and chess are other popular activities. Adults like to entertain friends and family, especially on weekends or holidays. During such get-togethers, people often enjoy singing

CHESS

karaoke. Some Filipino families take beach vacations during the summer. People also travel to visit relatives in various locations.

PLAY SIPA

Sipa is a traditional Filipino sport from the 1400s. Today it is played by children and adults. An informal game can be played anywhere. But games are also played on courts with nets.

What You Need:
- a metal washer
- colorful strings, ribbons, feathers, or rubber bands
- at least two players

Instructions:
1. Using the washer, create your own sipa. Weave whatever strings, ribbons, or rubber bands you choose through the middle of the washer.

2. One player kicks the sipa into the air to begin the game. Players use only the area from the foot until just above the knee to kick the sipa.

3. Players continue to kick the sipa. The goal is to make sure the sipa does not touch the ground. Each player must keep track to how many times they kick the sipa before it hits the ground.

4. The player who kicks the sipa the most times before the sipa hits the ground wins the game. Have fun!

FOOD

MENUDO   FRIED CHIX
POR STEAK CHIX BBQ
SISIG   CHIX CURRY
DINUGUA PASTEL
GINILING CADO
FRIED T
PANGA

ONE COOL, SWEET TREAT

Halo-halo, meaning "mix-mix" in Tagalog, is a popular Filipino dessert. This colorful treat contains shaved ice, condensed milk, fruits, and sweetened beans. Sometimes people even add cheese or cornflakes!

Rice is common in the Filipino diet. Cooks use rice in everything from main dishes to desserts. A common meal might be boiled rice, meat, cooked vegetables, and fruit. Fruit is also eaten for breakfast. Many Filipinos enjoy mangoes, custard apples, bananas, and durians.

A popular stew is *adobo*. It consists of chicken and pork cooked in soy sauce, garlic, and vinegar. *Kare-kare* is another favorite dish. Peanut sauce gives flavor to this vegetable and meat stew, which often contains oxtail. *Pancit palabok* is a rice noodle dish served with a sauce made from eggs, shrimp, and pork.

ADOBO

KARE-KARE

YEMA

Yema is a well-loved candy in the Philippines. It is sticky and sweet. Have an adult help you make this recipe.

Ingredients:

3 tablespoons unsalted butter
1 can (14 ounces) sweetened condensed milk
7 egg yolks

Steps:

1. Place the butter into a frying pan. Stir over medium heat until the butter is completely melted.

2. Pour the can of sweetened condensed milk into the pan. Add in the 7 egg yolks. Stir constantly using a rubber spatula or wooden spoon until the mixture bubbles slightly and becomes thick. This can take up to 15 minutes.

3. Pour the heated mixture onto a heatproof plate or baking sheet. Use your rubber spatula to spread the mixture into an even layer. Set the mixture aside to cool.

4. Use a butter knife to cut the cooled yema into about 16 squares or sections. Take one section at a time and roll it into a ball shape.

5. Place the finished balls on a plate. Enjoy!

People in the Philippines celebrate many holidays. New Year's fireworks displays start the year off with a bang on January 1. June 12 is Independence Day in the Philippines. On many islands, festivities include parades and fireworks.

MASSKARA FESTIVAL

Held in Bacolod City, the MassKara Festival takes place in October. The festival celebrates the strength of people in times of hardship. One big event is a street dance competition where participants wear smiling masks.

24

Christmas is the biggest holiday of the year. People commonly visit their hometowns during this season. People often start decorating, shopping, and listening to Christmas music in September. The season ends with a feast and visiting family on Three Kings' Day. Filipinos celebrate their **culture** and country throughout the year!

TIMELINE

1542
Spain claims and names the islands of the Philippines

1965
Ferdinand Marcos begins 20-year rule often filled with corruption

1898
The United States defeats Spain in the Spanish-American War and takes over the Philippines

1946
The Philippine Islands become fully independent as the Republic of the Philippines

1941
The Japanese take over the Philippines during World War II

1987
The present Constitution of the Philippines is approved

2014
Muslim rebel group Moro Islamic Liberation Front signs a peace deal with the Philippine government

2002
Multiple terrorist bomb attacks occur in Manila and Zamboanga City

1969
A guerrilla war begins between Muslim rebel groups and the Philippine government

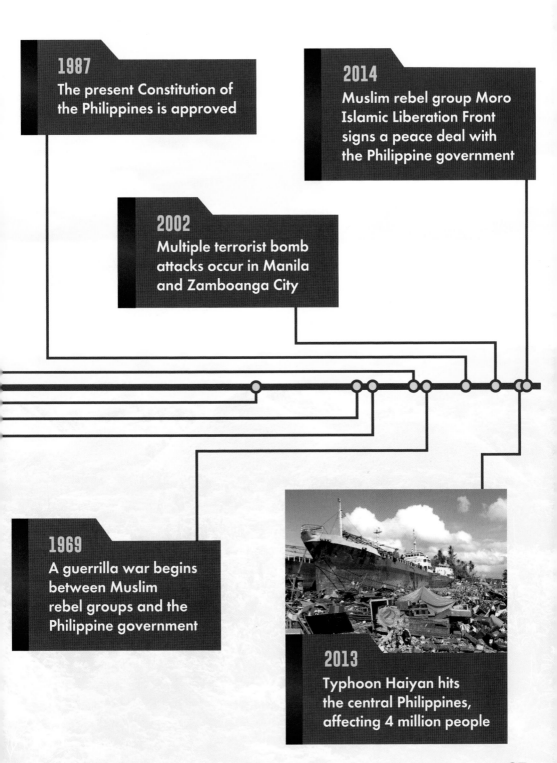

2013
Typhoon Haiyan hits the central Philippines, affecting 4 million people

PHILIPPINES FACTS

Official Name: Republic of the Philippines

Flag of the Philippines: The Philippines' flag has two horizontal bands. The top blue band represents justice and peace. The bottom red band stands for courage. A white triangle along the left side of the flag symbolizes equality. The yellow sun in the middle has eight rays. These rays represent the first eight provinces to seek independence. The small yellow stars represent the different island groups of the nation.

Area: 115,831 square miles (300,000 square kilometers)

Capital City: Manila

Important Cities: Davao, Cebu City, Zamboanga, Quezon City

Population:
109,180,815 (July 2020)

WHERE PEOPLE LIVE

COUNTRYSIDE
52.6%

CITY
47.4%

JOBS

- SERVICES **56.3%**
- MANUFACTURING **18.3%**
- FARMING **25.4%**

Main Exports:

computers

metals

minerals

vehicles

electronic parts

fruits and vegetables

National Holiday:
Independence Day (June 12)

Main Languages:
Filipino, English

Form of Government:
presidential republic

Title for Country Leader:
president

RELIGION

- PROTESTANT **8.2%**
- MUSLIM **5.6%**
- OTHER **5.6%**
- ROMAN CATHOLIC **80.6%**

Unit of Money:
Philippine peso

GLOSSARY

archipelago—a group of islands

coral reefs—structures made of coral that usually grow in shallow seawater

culture—the beliefs, arts, and ways of life in a place or society

dialects—local ways of speaking particular languages

ethnic—related to a group of people who share customs and an identity

karaoke—an activity in which people sing along to popular songs

mainland—a continent or main part of a continent

manufacture—to make products, often with machines

plains—large areas of flat land

primates—animals that use their hands to grasp food and other objects; primates are related to humans.

rain forests—thick, green forests that receive a lot of rain

rural—related to the countryside

sanctuary—a place of protection

service jobs—jobs that perform tasks for people or businesses

shantytowns—densely populated areas just outside a city that have poor living conditions and run-down housing

tourists—people who travel to visit another place

tradition—a custom, idea, or belief handed down from one generation to the next

tropical monsoonal—relating to a climate with high temperatures and rainfall that also has a short dry season

typhoons—powerful storms in the western Pacific Ocean

urban—related to cities and city life

vocational—involved in the training of a skill or trade that prepares an individual for a career

volcanoes—holes in the earth; when a volcano erupts, hot ash, gas, or melted rock called lava shoots out.

TO LEARN MORE

AT THE LIBRARY

Mattern, Joanne. *Philippines*. New York, N.Y.: Cavendish Square Publishing, 2018.

Mooney, Carla. *Traditional Stories of the Southeast Nations*. Minneapolis, Minn.: Core Library, 2018.

Yomtov, Nelson. *Immigrants from India and Southeast Asia*. North Mankato, Minn.: Capstone Press, 2018.

ON THE WEB

FACTSURFER

Factsurfer.com gives you a safe, fun way to find more information.

1. Go to www.factsurfer.com.

2. Enter "the Philippines" into the search box and click 🔍.

3. Select your book cover to see a list of related content.

INDEX

The images in this book are reproduced through the courtesy of: Rastro SK, front cover; valeriy eydlin,
pp. 4-5; Frolova_Elena, p. 5 (Banaue Rice Terraces); Edwin Verin, p. 5 (Hundred Islands National Park);
N8Allen, pp. 5 (Puerto-Princesa Subterranean River National Park), 15; suronin, p. 5 (San Agustin
Church); kokkai, p. 8; Marc_Osborne, p. 9 (top); r.nagy, p. 9 (bottom); Photoestetica, p. 10 (tarsier);
Ernie Janes/ Alamy, p. 9 (warty pig); Michael Bogner, p. 10 (tiger shark); Buiten-Beeld/ Alamy, p. 10
(flying frog); Arco Images GmbH/ Alamy, p. 11; Kobby Dagan, pp. 12, 24; ZUMA/ Alamy, p. 13 (top);
imwaltersy, p. 13 (bottom); Damian Pankowiec, p. 14; Scopio/ Alamy, p. 16; Peter Treanor/ Alamy,
p. 17; Danita Delimont/ Alamy, p. 18; Kim David, pp. 19 (top), 22 (halo-halo); Grant Rooney/ Alamy,
p. 19 (bottom); Stephane Bidouze, p. 20 (top); Farysa Hamzah, p. 20 (bottom); Pacific Press Agency/
Alamy, p. 21 (top); Art Phaneuf/ Alamy, p. 22; AS Food studio, p. 23 (top); bonchan, p. 23 (middle);
Goran Bogicevic, p. 23 (bottom); imagegallery2/ Alamy, p. 25; Archive PL/ Alamy, p. 26; ymphotos,
p. 27; Art-Studio/ Alamy, p. 29 (banknote); Fat Jackey, p. 29 (coin).